Dreamland

Primo

Shirley Mier

Favorite Duets from Alfred

(EE)..Early Elementary
(E) ....Elementary
(LE)... Late Elementary
(EI) Early Intermediate
(I) ....Intermediate
(LI)..Late Intermediate
(EA) ....Early Advanced
(A)..................Advanced

Celebrated Piano Duets (Vandall)

These books are new compilations of favorite Vandall duets complete with new engravings with careful attention to layout.

Book 1 (E/LE) ....22531 Book 4 (I)......................24551
Book 2 (LE/EI)..............22532 Book 5 (I/LI)..............24552
Book 3 (EI)....................22533

Classics for Piano Duet (Tingley)

This series offers beginners the opportunity to play the classics. By dividing the pieces between two performers, the parts are simplified, but the overall effect is rich and sparkling.

Book 1 (LE/EI) ....20773 Book 2 (EI/I)..............20774

Dances for Two (Rollin)

These duets capture the essence of dance music. Book 1 includes a French waltz, a jig, a tap dance, and a Baroque dance. Book 2 includes a Charleston, a polka, a Russian waltz, and a rock and roll dance. Book 3 includes a paso doble, big band swing, samba, and Broadway dance.

Book 1 (EI/I)..................19678 Book 3 (LI) 40579
Book 2 (I)......................19679

Duet Classics for Piano (Kowalchyk/Lancaster)

These unique volumes contain duets in their original form written by composers who lived in the 18th, 19th, and 20th centuries.

Book 1 (EI)....................6644 Book 3 (LI) 6646
Book 2 (I)......................6645

Duets for Animal Lovers (Goldston)

These indispensible collections add variety and help make practicing the piano become less work and more fun!

Duets for Bear Lovers (E)......................367
Duets for Cat Lovers (E).........................333
Duets for Dog Lovers (E) 334

Easy Classical Piano Duets
for Teacher and Student (Kowalchyk/Lancaster)

A valuable assortment of teacher/student duets in their original form written by teachers and composers during the 18th and 19th centuries. The student parts are limited to 5-finger position and fall primarily within the grand staff reading range.

Book 1 (E)..........................6507 Book 3 (E/LE)............16799
Book 2 (E)......................16789

Essential Keyboard Duets

These duets provide pianists the opportunity to become familiar with a broad range of literature and to experience well-known works in a more immediate and in-depth manner.

Volume 1 (LE/I) (Kowalchyk/Lancaster) 16747
Volume 2 (I/LI) (Kowalchyk/Lancaster) 20856

Volume 3 (I/EA) (Kowalchyk/Lancaster) 21439
Volume 4 (LI/EA) (Mauro/Beard) 32803
Volume 5 (LI/EA) (Mauro/Beard) 36433
Volume 6 (EA/A) (Kowalchyk/Lancaster) 36434
Volume 7 (EA/A) (Hinson/Nelson) 39348
Volume 8 (E/LE) (Kowalchyk/Lancaster) 37610

Famous & Fun Duets (Matz)

Famous & Fun Duets offer a wonderful introduction to timeless masterpieces and audience favorites. The arrangements include themes from symphonic, operatic, and keyboard literature.

Book 1 (EE)....................37033 Book 4 (EI) 37036
Book 2 (EE/E)..............37034 Book 5 (I)......................37037
Book 3 (E/LE) 37035

Famous & Fun Pop Duets (Matz)

This graded series contains popular hits from movies, radio, and TV. Each piece has been arranged especially for students of equal ability, while remaining faithful to the original.

Book 1 (EE)....................27705 Book 4 (EI) 28985
Book 2 (EE/E)..............27706 Book 5 (I)......................28986
Book 3 (E/LE) 27707

First Favorite Duets (Olson)

Easy 5-finger arrangements of the world's most popular melodies, designed to encourage independent reading. Duet accompaniments provide a fuller sound.

(E)..2588

Five-Star Duets (Alexander)

These colorful arrangements make it possible for elementary pianists to experience the joy of duet playing at the earliest opportunity. Both primo and secondo feature the melody and are equal in difficulty.

Christmas (E/LE)..........23233 Patriotic (LE)..............20776
Classical (LE)................21347 Sacred (LE)................21348
Folk (E)..........................19792

Grand Duets for Piano (Bober)

The thrill of making music with a friend or teacher is captured in this new series of duets. A variety of keys, styles, meters, and tempos are featured.

Book 1 (EE)..................32152 Book 4 (EI) 35440
Book 2 (E)......................32153 Book 5 (I)......................37114
Book 3 (LE)..................35439 Book 6 (LI) 37115

Jazz, Rags & Blues for Two (Mier)

The magic of Martha Mier's Jazz, Rags & Blues is back in this series–Jazz, Rags & Blues for Two. Enjoy the syncopated rhythms, colorful sounds, and rich harmonies of jazz in a variety of styles.

Book 1 (EI)....................21386 Book 4 (LI/EA)..........22455
Book 2 (I)......................21387 Book 5 (EA)................38829
Book 3 (I/LI)..................22454

Just for Two (Alexander)

The solo piano series, Just for You, was one of Dennis Alexander's first and best-selling series with Alfred. In Just for Two, Dennis has created duet versions of many favorites from each book of the original series. Students will enjoy making music together with these duets that are "twice the fun" as the originals.

Book 1 (EE/E) ....39103 Book 3 (I)......................39105
Book 2 (EI)....................39104 Book 4 (I/LI)..............39106

Just for You & Me (Alexander)

Syncopation, singing melodies, tender ballads, mixed meters, and mellow contemporary sounds are all found in this collection, designed to provide hours of musical enjoyment.

Book 1 (LE/EI) ....6657 Book 2 (LE/EI)..............6658

Kaleidoscope Duets (George)

These books introduce the student to a wide variety of musical designs and colors that spark the imagination while developing technical skills.

Book 1 (E)..........................691 Book 4 (EI/I)..................697
Book 2 (LE/EI) ....692 Book 5 (I)......................698
Book 3 (EI)........................693

Masterwork Classics Duets
(Kowalchyk/Lancaster/Magrath)

These graded collections of piano duets by master composers are among the best literature available at respective levels. Each duet, written by composers who lived in the 18th, 19th, or 20th century, has been carefully edited and fingered for performance ease.

Book 1 (E)......................40836 Book 3 (LE/EI)............40838
Book 2 (E/LE) ....40837 Book 4 (EI/I)..............40839

Music for Sharing (Goldston)

The wide variety of styles presented in these books are perfect for recitals, sight-reading, or just for fun!

Book 1 (EE)....................11716 Book 2 (E) 11717

Terrific Tunes for Two (Mier)

The duets in Terrific Tunes for Two will encourage students to play with imagination. Both the primo and secondo parts are written at an equal level of difficulty.

Book 1 (E/LE) ....17394 Book 2 (LE/EI)............17395

Treasures for Two (Mier)

These two volumes each contain six captivating duets in various styles including blues, jazz, ragtime, and even a tango! Both the primo and secondo parts are written at the same level of difficulty.

Book 1 (EI/I)..................11753 Book 2 (I/LI) 11754

47082 $4.99 in USA

ISBN 1-4706-4040-6

alfred.com

ISBN-10: 1-4706-4040-6
ISBN 13: 978-1-4706-4040-8